THE AUTHORITY GUIDE TO
PROFITABLE
PRICING

How to develop a powerful strategy to boost
turnover, profit, cash flow and business growth

SHAZ NAWAZ

The Authority Guide to Profitable Pricing
How to develop a powerful strategy to boost
turnover, profit, cash flow and business growth
© Shaz Nawaz

ISBN 978-1-912300-10-5
eISBN 978-1-912300-11-2

Published in 2017 by Authority Guides
authorityguides.co.uk

Contents

Pricing is actually pretty simple...
Customers will not pay literally a penny
more than the true value of the product.

Ron Johnson

Introduction

This book is aimed at those professionals who are owners of, or who control pricing in, businesses of any size, worldwide.

Pricing is, in my opinion, *the* most neglected and misunderstood area of business operation, yet it's certainly one of the most important. The biggest and quickest gains I've seen among my clients have involved developing a better and smarter pricing strategy.

People in business are constantly making endless mistakes with their pricing – and keep repeating those mistakes. This book shows you in-depth how to get this crucial aspect of your business right.

Incorrect pricing is holding the great majority of businesses back, to the extent of being a main factor contributing to financial failure in many cases. The majority of small and medium enterprises in particular don't have a proper pricing policy – and don't really know what the product or service they sell is worth. Getting pricing right can produce an immediate increase in turnover and profitability, greatly widening options and triggering expansion and growth.

So the majority of businesses are suffering through non-optimal pricing. The need for a more effective approach to pricing applies not only to recent or new start-ups, but equally to most established businesses. This book is for those who are daunted by the subject of pricing, those who know they have a problem with it – and those whose businesses are simply not as profitable as they ought to be.

The Authority Guide to Profitable Pricing takes the reader through the major mistakes that so many businesses are making in their pricing, and sets out a clear and practical approach to optimum pricing that can enable an immediate increase in profitability.

Business is a game of margins. Yet most businesses tend to work on overly tight margins due to having an ineffective pricing strategy. The truth of the matter is that most businesses don't really spend any time on their pricing strategy – at worst it's a 'finger-in-the-air' job, and at best it's often merely an analysis of the range of prices which competitors charge, then pitching somewhere in the middle of that.

This book will help you to understand how to devise in detail a highly profitable pricing strategy; you'll learn a step-by-step process that will help you to charge what you're actually worth.

In this book, we're talking about a major potential shift in what and how you think about yourself. Much of my time is spent getting people to stop undervaluing themselves; this is not a good basis for healthy pricing.

How to use the book

There are four possible approaches to getting the learning you need to improve your pricing strategies and gain the corresponding advantages for your business from this book:

- Read it from start to finish if you really haven't thought about pricing strategy too deeply to date, or if the whole subject flummoxes you. This will give you a 'big picture' view of this complex subject.

- Read individual chapters that relate to specific issues, if you're generally savvy about pricing but know that there are certain issues which need addressing, or areas that you have neglected thinking about in your pricing strategies. Cross-referencing between the chapters will help you to find related content if you adopt this more focused approach.

- Browse through and see what piques your interest, if that's the kind of person you are – maybe select your most favourite chapter, then read your next most favourite (I'm one of this type of business book readers).

- Speed read the whole book and then return to the chapters that you now consider you need to study in detail, those relevant to you and your business at this particular point in time, or which cover blind spots in your historical approach to pricing.

Whichever approach you adopt, I encourage you not to make the mistake of skipping chapters or parts of chapters that you may think of as unimportant, or that might seem too abstract, or that deal with underlying principles rather than practical steps – such as the chapters on positioning or mindset, which are probably the most important chapters of all. Most readers will benefit from the radical overhaul of habitual ways of thinking and assumptions about pricing, which this book offers.

Please also don't just read the book and put it away – as you read, make notes of actions you can take, and then use these to create an action plan. Then put this plan into practice! That's how you're really going to benefit from this book.

What the book covers

There's logic in the way the book is laid out, and in the sequencing of information – so reading it in this order is advantageous if you want a comprehensive and thorough grounding in the subject.

Chapter 1 spells out in detail why pricing is so fundamentally important to business success, and why you need to think about pricing – and probably rethink it – in a profound way.

Chapter 2 demonstrates how central pricing is to your business figures – margins, cash flow and profit – and explains how the subtle mechanisms of these relationships work.

Chapter 3 lists the most common mistakes and pitfalls that occur in business pricing. There's a good chance that something you're doing right now is in this chapter.

Chapter 4 explains the variety of forms and options for applying pricing in your business, explaining the merits of each system and where they're best used, and enabling you to work out which options are most suitable for you and your business.

Chapter 5 tackles the hugely important question of what is going on in the mind of a person who could be about to spend money with you, and how understanding this can help you to positively alter their perception of what you have to offer – and clinch deals.

In Chapter 6 we look at the issue of competitiveness in matters related to pricing – it's not just about competing on price, but all aspects of how to position yourself competitively in your marketplace.

Chapter 7 gives you guidance on how you can use guarantees to get more business through increasing the customer's confidence in spending money with you.

Chapter 8 delves deeply into the game-changing matter of how some companies position themselves to be world leaders in their field and as a consequence reap huge business success as a result – and how you can apply the same principles in your own business setting.

Price is what you pay. Value is what you
get.

Warren Buffet

1. Why price matters

In my experience, when people set up a new business, they pay a lot of attention to matters such as:

- The nature of their core product, service or business offering
- Renting the right office
- Staffing
- Office paper letterhead and stationery
- Advertising
- Website and social media

However, what I find time and again is that new businesses – and established businesses, too – pay little attention to their pricing. Their means of arriving at prices is often cursory in the extreme – they may do a web search to see what other companies are charging for something similar, see what is the highest and the lowest, and use somewhere in the middle to come up with their price.

This is despite the fact that, in nine cases out of ten, if you ask the owner of such a company whether their product or service has any distinctive or even unique qualities, they will not hesitate in saying yes and will also start listing them. Yet the pricing they have does not represent this distinctiveness – representing a massive wasted opportunity. You might as well write on your website, 'You can see from our pricing that there is nothing distinctive about what we want to sell to you.'

Another pricing strategy that I come across frequently with new companies, in particular where an individual has struck out on their own after working with another company, is making sure that they price their offering lower than their old boss's. They do this in an effort to gain a competitive advantage and take business away from the other company, whose set-up they know very well.

Both these approaches are wrong – they are simplistic, misguided and ineffective. I'll show you why as you read through the chapters of this book.

Pricing for new and established businesses

Once a new business is established, the owner may soon start to think, 'How can I get more customers?' A less than optimum level of pricing may be somewhat more understandable when you're new in the field, but once you become established it is absolutely crucial to get your price right and improve your margins. I find, time after time, that once a business is established the owner will begin to realise that:

- the intentions and projections in their original business plan are not being reflected in where they are now
- bank balance and cash flow statements are not reflecting the position the owner had hoped for
- profitability is lower than expected.

So it is at this point that the owner is likely to be more open to acknowledging that the pricing is not right.

In this book, I will show you that it is a lot easier to adjust your pricing in order to get it right for maximum profit, rather than only making a big effort to win many more customers, which takes a great deal of time, effort and money. The ideal scenario for a new business, of course, is to get the pricing right from the outset, thus getting your customers used to your optimum prices from the beginning. And, of course, this is all the more urgent for established businesses of any size.

So being fixated on getting new customers, as an activity pursued on its own, does not make any sense – far better to see it as an integrated natural outcome of getting your pricing policy right and reaping the wide range of benefits that can flow from this.

The subject of getting the price right in relation to the effect on your margins is covered in-depth in Chapter 2.

Attracting the right customer

But it's not just about your margins and your cash flow and your profitability – getting your price right means getting the right type of customer, which is perhaps the most central issue in any business – and one that I often find neglected. If your prices are too low, you will tend to attract the wrong kind of customer, the kind of customer that's not good for your business – one who just looks for the cheapest and is not so interested in getting their needs met by an offering that delivers real benefits.

Take a customer, for instance, who buys a Casio watch – this person will differ in crucial ways from one who will buy a Rolex watch. The Casio customer may well only possess one watch, and mainly owns it in order to know the time – and will want it to last as long as possible so as not to have to spend money on a replacement.

A Rolex customer, on the other hand, buys a watch partly in order to know the time, but more importantly as a value statement about who they are. This type of customer wants to get additional benefits from the purchase – and for this reason can deliver much more significant benefits to the business who sells the watch. For instance:

- they will be willing to pay £500 or maybe even £20,000 for the product
- they are likely to buy more than one watch, and may become a collector
- they will be happier to pay for servicing and supplementary purchases because they want their watch to hold its high value
- owning a product like this gives them 'bragging rights', so they will be giving word of mouth appreciation and publicity to their friends, which will benefit the supplier of these products
- they may well also talk about their new purchase and show a picture of it on social media – which they're not going to do with a Casio, are they?

This is why the most successful and highly profitable companies in the world are those who are well known for offering a premium product at a premium price – think Apple, Harrods, Gucci, Rolls-Royce, private jet companies, yacht companies and other premium or luxury suppliers.

So that, in a nutshell, is the difference between the kind of customer you want and the kind you don't want – and how you can price accordingly, because optimum pricing demonstrates that you understand the value of your offering to your customer. We will look into this important distinction in customer mindset in more detail in Chapter 5. The closely related issue of how you position yourself relative to others in your marketplace is explored in-depth in Chapter 8.

Other issues affected by pricing

Optimum pricing also enables you to enhance other important aspects of your business, which in turn support more sales, more turnover and more profit. This can mean, for instance, that:

- you can employ better staff
- you can give a better service to your customers
- your customers will stay longer with you, make more purchases and spend more money with you
- your customers are more likely to refer other customers to you, and these will be like-minded people, who are your best kind of customer.

If you ask most businesses where they get most new customers, the most common answer is 'Word of mouth!' So new customers brought in by existing customers will already have been desensitised about paying a somewhat higher price, because they will have been told by their friend that you are not the cheapest, but that they are happy with the sale and have benefited from it. They are not expecting you to be cheap, and they will be happy to accept what you are charging. Wouldn't we all like more customers like that?

Improved pricing enables you to spend more on customer service, and deliver a better experience to each of your customers. So if you are charging the right price and making a good profit, then you have better margins from which to spend more on marketing – and find more of the right kind of customer.

Once you have attracted these additional customers, you will be in a position to spend more per customer on customer service – to do more for them, to wow them and keep them happy with extra value, and keep them for longer. This will then create more profit for you to continue to expand and to find still more such customers. It's a win–win situation, and an upward spiral.

What bad pricing does for you

Getting pricing wrong on the other hand, in particular by pricing too low, brings a whole range of downsides, which together tend to have a progressively downward spiralling effect on your business. This can mean for example:

- making less profit
- having poorer cash flow, and going to the bank manager for overdraft facilities
- Making it harder to attract and keep good staff, and pay them properly
- paying your own suppliers late, which can mean getting less favourable rates from them
- working for longer hours
- creating strain in your family and home life

All of this will also lead you towards not paying yourself what you are worth. I find that a majority of business owners, at the end of the month, just take out what's left over after everything else has been paid, rather than what they feel they really need. This is not only bad for you and your family, for your life and your stress patterns – it will have an adverse effect on the overall functioning of your business and your ability to attract new customers. This psychological phenomenon will also have a profound knock-on effect: if you're not paying yourself what you're worth, why would other people (your customers) value you and what you're offering?

Getting pricing wrong brings other problems, too, such as:

- low pricing attracts those customers already mentioned, who are excessively sensitive to pricing rather than other criteria

- if those customers come to you on the basis of low pricing, they will leave you just as readily when they can find a similar offering being sold just a little cheaper

- being cheap actually gives you no competitive advantage, unless you happen to be Amazon or Walmart

- competing with other companies on low price is a race to the bottom – it makes no sense. There will always be someone cheaper than you.

These and other pricing pitfalls are looked at in detail in Chapter 3. Competitive pricing is important, but is by no means a matter of just being lower than everyone else. A detailed examination of the options can be found in Chapter 6.

Conclusion

In my experience, not getting pricing right is the single most common reason for the fact that a great majority of new businesses close down or go bankrupt in their first five years of operation.

So we can see that pricing is fundamentally important to the whole success of your business, its surviving and its thriving – and quite probably to your own personal wellbeing and happiness, too. Pricing must not be just an afterthought; it is key to everything in your business.

Please go to the website that accompanies this book at shaznawaz.co.uk/pricingresources for 20 practical comparative worksheets on how to optimise your pricing.

2. Pricing and numbers

Business is a game of margins. In this chapter, I'm going to show you how important your pricing strategy is in optimising the key numbers and figures in your business offering.

To have a business that is going to be sustainable in the present and into the future, you obviously need to be profitable. In order to make sure you generate a profit, you need to know how all the key numbers are stacking up, and you need to make sure you are making decent margins. You need to be monitoring these margins on a regular basis.

Unfortunately, what I find is that most businesses don't keep a good handle on their numbers or their margins, and consequently get into trouble before long.

The little-understood mechanism of price effect on margins

Many business professionals realise that increasing price will have an effect on raising margins and profitability, but do not grasp exactly how this mechanism works – and precisely how advantageous or disadvantageous pricing steps can have. Here's how it can work.

The beauty of a price *increase* is that it goes straight to your bottom line, rather than being eroded by other countering costs. This is illustrated in Figure 1.

Figure 1 The effect of price change on profit

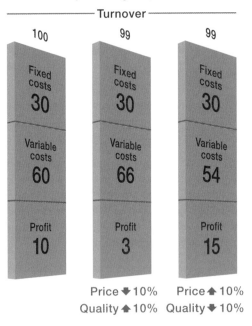

Column 1 (left-hand side) shows the starting position. Column 2 illustrates what happens when the price is reduced by 10 per cent and the quantity sold increases by 10 per cent. Overall the business makes less profit: £3 instead of £10.

Column 3 illustrates what happens when the price increases by 10 per cent and the quantity sold decreases by 10 per cent.

The profit equates to £15, which is a 50 per cent increase from where we started, in column 1.

For instance, if your turnover is £50,000 per year and your total costs are £40,000 per annum, then your profit would be £10,000. This would represent a 20 per cent net margin – which would be regarded as adequate by many businesses.

If you were then to increase your price by 5 per cent, your turnover would now be £52,500, but your costs would remain at £40,000, so your profit would be £12,500 – an increase of 25 per cent on your net profit margin – equal to five times the price increase. So a small increase of 5 per cent has a disproportionately greater effect on net margin.

However, in the marketplace I find that there is a general misconception that if you drop your price you'll get more customers and therefore will be able to make more money overall. So let's look at an example of how *that* mechanism works, illustrated in Figure 1.

If you drop your price by 5 per cent, for instance, then your turnover would become £47,500, and your net profit would then be £7,500 – which is down 25 per cent; so you would need an additional 25 per cent volume in sales to achieve this – working 25 per cent harder, just to get to the same point where you are now.

An increase on this scale – suddenly finding 25 per cent more customers – is not at all easy to do. It will cost you a lot of money on marketing and advertising to get this many more customers, so in fact that number would not keep you at the same level of margin: you would then need an even greater increase, just to preserve your margins – perhaps 35 or 40 per cent more customers than you previously had, which would be very challenging.

To achieve this you would probably have to cut corners – typically on customer service or marketing spend. These are generally the least desirable areas to cut back on; not only would you attract less business, you would not be looking after your existing customers, who are then likely to go elsewhere.

If you cut your marketing budget, which is the first thing many businesses do in these circumstances, then you are not winning new customers, and not growing your business. Or if you choose to cut your training budget, another popular choice in such cases, then the quality of your service will deteriorate as you are not keeping staff and their skills up to date, and you may lose staff who leave to join a business that better supports their ongoing professional development.

Furthermore, being cheaper also tells your existing and potential customers that your product or service is probably inferior – whereas being more expensive tells them that you are likely to be superior. If you have reduced your prices, people will ask themselves why you've become cheaper; they will wonder what's going on. We live in a sceptical world – after all, it's only retailers that put on 'sales'. Your customers are people who will make such assumptions based on how they see things – their perceived reality. This aspect of customer mindset and perception is explored in much more depth in Chapter 5.

So the option of reducing your prices with a view to getting more customers can be a very bad idea all round.

Higher markup items

Another example of how price effect can be used to advantage rather than disadvantage lies in selling some items that have a higher markup, even if they may not sell so often or in such numbers. Every business usually has a few product or service items that make really good margins, in addition to their more standard offering.

For instance, if a lawnmower company sells both cheaper and more expensive models, then they also sell other products such as first year servicing, or lawnmower tools, accessories and add-ons, which usually produce higher margins than the bulk sale items.

Amazon is an excellent example of a company that does this very well – they look at what their customers everywhere are doing and will tell you 'people who bought this also bought a, b and c' – and these are often items that deliver higher margins to the company. People are often most at ease when they are just in the buying process – so the best time to sell them something new is when they've just bought something else. They are motivated, they're in the process of buying, and they have temporarily overcome their resistance to spending their money, so you can take advantage of that. Amazon have shown that people are open to guidance in this way, so you too can play a role in guiding your customers towards that type of objective. This can involve selling them additional components that have a low inherent cost to you, but a high perceived value to the customer – thus improving your margin.

Examples of this type of item can also include warranties, after-sales care products or six-month check-ups; companies like John Lewis often provide a three-year warranty where others only offer one year. Accountants might offer to handle enquiries from the tax authorities on behalf of their customer in addition to regular bookkeeping and accounts, at low cost, or included in the original price of the service. Furniture retailers are masters of this. The markup on a sofa selling at, say, £2,000 would typically be 35 per cent, whereas the markup on aftercare costing £50 is more likely to be around 70 per cent.

Responding to higher costs

What happens if one of your suppliers increases their costs? How you respond to this is another important aspect that must be properly taken into account in your pricing strategy. Table 1 is an example of the effects of this mechanism at work.

Table 1 The effect of supplier cost increase

	Before	After	Required result
Turnover	1,500,000	1,600,000	1,650,000
Purchase costs	1,000,000	1,100,000	1,110,000
Markup (%)	50.00	45.45	33.33
Gross profit	500,000	500,000	550,000
Gross profit (%)	33.33	31.25	33.33

This example illustrates what happens if your supplier increases their prices by 10 per cent, together with the effect of you making a price increase to cover the additional cost of purchasing the stock i.e. 100,000 increase, and the fact that you actually need to make an overall increase of 10 per cent (on your turnover) to preserve your existing margin, as shown in the required result column. What sometimes happens is that the retailer only passes on the increase from their supplier. This is not sufficient to retain margins. You must actually increase your selling price by the same percentage in order to maintain your overall margins.

Conclusion

It is highly advisable for you to track margins on all your product and service lines on a monthly basis, and from there set targets for your overall growth margins, then ensure that you are working towards those through your pricing strategy. Be extremely wary of cutting your prices as a sole measure to gain more clients, and consider raising your prices and adding high markup items to your range.

If you get your pricing and therefore your margins right, everything else in your business will more easily fall into place. But if you don't do your monitoring, you won't know what your current margins are – and when your accountant analyses your figures at the end of the financial year, it will be too late to do anything retrospectively.

Interactive spreadsheets that you can use to apply the recommendations in this chapter to the figures for your own business are available online at the website for this book, shaznawaz.co.uk/pricingresources

If you cannot get it all right, don't get it all wrong.

Ernest Agyemang Yeboah

3. Common pricing pitfalls and how to avoid them

In this chapter, I'm going to tell you about the seven most common and damaging mistakes that can be made in pricing strategy and execution. I encounter each of these time and again amongst my clients and in my talks and seminars. These pitfalls are having devastating effects on businesses all around the world, causing all kinds of problems from cash flow to closure and bankruptcy.

Pitfall 1: pricing self-sabotage

Most business owners think price is the absolute number one factor in the mind of every person who might buy from them but, generally speaking, this is not true – price is *a* factor, but not *the* factor. Granted, a certain limited percentage of people will always buy the cheapest, and again there is a certain percentage who will always buy the best or most expensive quality available, but apart from these minorities, the great majority of purchasers in the marketplace will be guided in their purchasing choices by a complex combination of different reasons.

Let's look at just one particular market area. If we think about customers buying a holiday, then it will be immediately obvious that the factors taken into account by the great majority of buyers in their purchase choice will probably include:

- the category of airline they choose to fly with, for example no-frills or upmarket
- the class they regularly choose, for example first class, business or economy
- the choice of particular day or particular time they wish to travel
- the type and quality of hotel they wish to stay in
- the kind of resort or location they want to go to, whether it provides them with the opportunity for lying on a beach, deep-sea diving or studying the habitat of a rare and endangered beetle in the jungles of New Guinea
- all kinds of other personal preferences such as climate and weather, social preferences, or aesthetic choices, and what class of people they wish or don't wish to be mingling with.

So each individual will prioritise some or other of these criteria, and will therefore be prepared to pay what it takes to get what they want, while the other factors will be less important to them, and they will choose the lowest price available in relation to those. It's certainly not true that everybody wants the cheapest option against all of these criteria.

Thinking that everyone wants the cheapest and then basing your pricing strategy on that is the worst type of self-sabotage. This is because in order to keep your price down you will have a negative impact on many aspects of what you deliver in order to keep your costs down, with all kinds of knock-on effects. One of the worst effects of this is that you yourself will become 'cheap' – you are not valuing yourself and what you offer, and therefore others will not value you either.

Many sellers, working hard to make their offering the best it can be, believe that they are better than their competition – yet charge the same price or even a lower price than those competitors, but do not see the lack of congruence in this state of affairs. You have to make what you're selling valuable, and then you've got to believe that it's valuable and determine your price strategy accordingly.

People who think cheap believe that if they increase their prices they will be worse off, but it is more often than not the opposite case. Generally speaking, if you increase your prices and take appropriate accompanying measures, then you are likely to be better off. The trick is to position yourself so that you are seen as a premium provider, and to add more value to what you are offering so that you can charge the higher price.

So instead of asking ourselves what is the lowest price we can charge in order to attract more business, our question should be, 'What is the maximum amount of value that I can give my customer for every pound or dollar that they spend with me?' This is a completely different and immensely more empowering way of looking at the whole process, and it will lead to more value added, more trust from the customer and thus more customers buying from you – at a higher price than you would otherwise be charging.

This is covered in more detail in Chapter 5.

Pitfall 2: being out of touch and pricing too high

Just as self-sabotage by too low pricing is a pitfall, so also is the opposite tendency – another form of being out of touch with reality – incorrectly thinking your product or service is better than anyone else's, and therefore pricing too high for the demand. Customers will just not be prepared to pay a premium price if their purchase does not bring them a premium outcome. I know of a number of companies who were mid-range or exclusive and have had to go into administration. These include household names like Austin Reed, Nicole Farhi, Serene (clothing retailer) and Jane Norman (ladies fashion retailer). This goes to show that the price has to reflect the value.

No business is immune from giving less and charging more. In fact, it's the opposite, as you have to give more than what you charge for – that's what's expected nowadays. However, the extra that you give doesn't always have to be the kitchen sink – it's small added touches that are appreciated by the customer but don't cost you much to deliver.

The once very successful Woolworths chain is a particularly familiar example. The decision makers there failed to understand where the market was moving and change with the times. They stayed just where they had always been in terms of pricing strategy and market position, while their customers were changing their expectations. As a result they went belly up. Had they added value and priced accordingly, they could have survived.

Such complacency is a big, deep pitfall.

Pitfall 3: fixating on price alone

Fixation on price – and only price – is another big pitfall if you're not careful. Your business and pricing strategy need to be much broader than this, integrating pricing policy with all the other aspects of business strategy. To this end you need to look at all the relevant issues, and ask yourself questions such as:

- What does your customer really want? You need a very clear understanding on this most important issue.

- Why do you exist in the marketplace? For instance, what do you offer that nobody else offers?

- Why should people buy from you rather than from someone else?

- What part of the market are you targeting; for instance, is it the premium market or the mass market? Are you an Apple or a Lidl, an easyJet or a Harrods? In other words, know where your natural place is in the marketplace and price accordingly.

- How good is your customer service?

- How efficient is your operation?

Pitfall 4: the wrong attitude

A big problem that I've encountered in very many businesses, and one that is causing them huge pricing problems, is that nearly all businesses think their set-up is different from everyone else's, and therefore that everything they do has to be unique to them.

When teaching pricing strategy or recommending a particular pricing approach to a client, I very often receive the reply, 'But my business is different, so this is not going to work for me' – or they may say, 'But we've always done it *this* way.' To which you might reply, 'If you keep on doing what you're doing, you'll keep on getting what you're getting.' They might be selling food or cars or delivering training or making spatulas for non-stick frying pans – it doesn't matter; all businesses are basically the same, apart from two particular aspects: the product or service they are offering, and the individual who is running the business. In all other aspects, they have the same needs and they must conform to the same requirements. They all need to perform the same basic business functions: sales, marketing, operations, finance, human resources and so on.

The right attitude leads someone starting a new business to work out a proper pricing strategy based on how to make the business profitable, have a good margin and ensure that the pricing reflects the quality of the offering. But instead, many people in business either simply set their price below their competitors, or look at what everyone else is charging and set their price to either the cheapest or midway between the highest and lowest.

Both these strategies are dangerous, because there is no regard to the margins generated from selling the product or service, and there is no account taken of the fact that operations and overheads at the outset will probably not be streamlined. These people are generally thinking about their competitors: 'By pricing this way, I'll take all their customers' – or else they're just taking a chance on the whole thing rather than approaching it with joined-up thinking. This is, in large part, why 80 per cent of new businesses fail in their first five years – because they simply didn't give proper consideration to margins, profit and cash flow – and so businesses simply aren't able to sustain themselves.

So I encourage you, too, to think in this way: 'What else can I do, which may work equally well in my business? And how can I test pricing in keeping with this experimentation?' Large retailers are notorious for using this approach, regularly pushing their boundaries and using different models for pricing such as buy-one-get-one-free, free delivery for online purchases and so on. In small businesses, it is essential for your survival and your success that you look at things in this same creative way.

Pitfall 5: not understanding your customer

If you as a business owner don't understand your customer, then there will inevitably be misconceptions about what your customer is going to buy from you – and what they will be willing to pay.

Alongside this, many businesses I encounter will proudly say, 'Our product is one of the best in the marketplace' – yet when you look at their pricing you can find that it can be very much lower than many of their competitors who are offering similar quality, or equal to those who are offering lower quality.

The million-dollar question is this: 'What is your customer thinking when they look at your price?' If your price is low, are they thinking 'There must be something inferior about this offering, otherwise why would it be offered at such a low price?' The old adage, which will inevitably be going through their minds, is that 'You get what you pay for.'

Remember this: you will probably not have done the wide-ranging price research that your customer has done, who, aided by a simple online search, will often have looked very closely at exactly who is offering what in terms of your precise product type and price range.

In addition to price, there are many factors that come into play and which buyers consider. For most clients price is *a* factor but not *the* factor. So the key point is that if you truly believe you have a quality offering, then you must make sure that your price reflects that – otherwise you're going to be leaving a whole lot of money on the table.

The trick is never to base your pricing on trying to second-guess what the customer will be willing to pay – the only reliable way to find out is to actually test it in the marketplace.

Pitfall 6: not testing your pricing thoroughly enough

Most businesses don't do nearly enough testing of pricing options in the marketplace. Many of those I speak to tell me, 'I increase my prices in line with inflation' – and many haven't put their prices up in many years. But if you're not increasing your prices often enough, you're diminishing your margin because you're going to be paying out more, but not passing that extra cost on.

A less obvious mistake is where sellers do pass on the increasing costs, but just pass on the increase itself. For instance, let's say you're buying a gizmo for £1.00 and selling it for £1.50 – a 50 per cent markup. If the cost to you increases by 10p to £1.10 and you pass that on by selling at £1.60, then you no longer have a 50 per cent markup: it will now be 45.45 per cent – a reduction of nearly 10 per cent. That's exactly what a very large number of businesses do – they haven't really thought it through. (Please refer to Table 1 on page 14.)

If your markup goes down by this much, then your gross profit margin will go down from 33.33 per cent to 31.25 per cent on each sale. Extrapolating this to scale of selling, let's say you're selling one million of these gizmos – then you're looking at a gross profit drop of 6.2 per cent.

What you should do instead, to preserve your margins and profit percentages, is to add on 15p instead of 10p to each sale. If you increase your price by only 10 per cent then you've compromised on your markup and on your gross profit margin (as stated above). However, your actual gross profit would remain the same. In our example it would remain at £500,000. If, however, you increased your price by 15p then your markup would remain the same, that is, 50 per cent, your gross profit percentage would remain the same, that is, 33.33 per cent and your actual gross profit would increase to £550,000 – this would give you an increase of £50,000 in your gross profit. And that is the way to manage price increases from suppliers. Never ever compromise your existing margins unless you fully understand your numbers and are willing to accept a reduction in your margins.

What you really need to do, though, is to test out your prices till you find your 'magic price'. This is illustrated in Figure 2.

Figure 2 The magic price

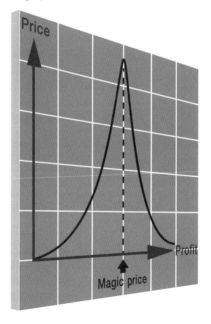

You'll never know the optimal price at which you should sell your products or service. Why? Because ultimately you wouldn't have tested your prices enough to find out. So the only way to establish the optimal price is to test different price points. In doing so you'll get to a stage where a particular price enables you to achieve maximum profit. That price is known as your *magic price*.

If you charge below your magic price number then you'll be losing profit because you're too cheap. If you charge more than your magic price then you'll be losing profit again because not enough people will be buying from you. Figure 2 illustrates this simple yet profound principle.

Pitfall 7: the fear factor

The fear I am referring to here is this: 'If I increase my prices, my customers will disappear.' I hear this fear expressed all the time. It's a dangerous concept, which is based on the assumption that all your customers joined you solely on the basis of you being the cheapest, which will not be true unless you are the absolute lowest in the whole of your marketplace.

The second reason why it's a dangerous concept is that this fear is based on the assumption that all of your customers are so disloyal and fickle that they will leave you in droves purely because of a price rise. This is highly unlikely to be the case; customers know that prices have to rise. The problem is that many sellers don't!

So don't buy into this irrational fear – all of your customers are not going to run away en masse; and if a few do, they will be the worst customers, who cost you the most to provide for and deal with. In the business we call these customers the BMWs: bitchers, moaners and whingers. They spend their time BMW-ing about your prices, your services, your quality and your timelines – and anything going wrong in *their* business is *your* fault. So you can think to yourself, 'Good riddance to bad margins!'

Furthermore, if you increase your price by 2 per cent, then lose 5 per cent of your customers – your worst customers – you're still making more money. Then you don't have to deal with those customers who were costing you money and time; and you're not working as hard, because you're serving 5 per cent less customers. Simple!

Conclusion

The main point behind all this is that if you don't truly value yourself and your offering, then why should anyone else? So be bold, be brave and have the confidence to test your prices – and your price increases.

Wealth isn't about money. It's about options... and you always have options. Choose wisely. Live wealthy.

Richie Norton

4. Different pricing options

There is a very wide range of business pricing forms from which to choose the best option for the different circumstances that may arise in your business. In this chapter, we'll look at the most popular options, what types of business use them, their pros and cons, and when they will be appropriate.

Cost-plus pricing

The pricing system used by the great majority of people in business is *cost-plus pricing*, which is based on simple markup. This pricing is based on ascertaining what it costs you to make a particular product or to deliver a particular service, then adding a standardised markup amount. But just because it's the most popular system doesn't mean it's the best.

The first challenge that comes up with cost-plus is that most businesses don't know how much it costs them to deliver something. In my experience, a lot of businesses don't even know what their net profit is!

However, an even bigger drawback with simple cost-plus pricing is that, as the name implies, it focuses exclusively on cost, rather than on the value given to the customer – in other words, on the production process rather than on the results – which is what the customer is really interested in, and which is the key outcome of your business from an enlightened business point of view.

This approach is ineffective because it misses out on the need and the opportunity to cover by price the real value provided to the customer. This results in two potential situations, both unsatisfactory. If your business is working inefficiently, then you will be overcharging the customer for the quality that they are receiving; whereas if you are operating efficiently, then you will be selling at too low a price. In either scenario, you and your customers become incompatible, your relationship with them is unsustainable and things will go wrong. If this continues, then either your customers will leave you or you will go out of business.

Another way of putting this is that cost-plus pricing creates a *production mentality* – an effect holding back your entrepreneurial thinking and capability. If you become more efficient, and reduce how much it costs you to deliver, then you are likely to reduce your price and you will be punishing yourself for efficiency. What incentive is there then to become more efficient? Also, if you're highly inefficient, you're charging customers more – why should they pay more because you can't get your house in order? In both these scenarios, both you and your customers become incompatible. Either way, one of you will be worse off.

Cost-plus pricing likewise penalises advances, such as technological improvements.

In other words, I very much advise that your pricing be based on how much value you are delivering rather than on how much it costs to deliver it. This is discussed in the next section.

Another hazard is that with cost-plus your rates are set by the marketplace and by your competitors rather than by you, which takes away your power to control your business and its outcomes. One of the key problems here is that it doesn't allow you to differentiate yourself from those competitors.

Perhaps the main problem with cost-plus can be expressed as the fact that it limits potential income; you can only increase your income by spending more and more on sales and marketing to find more customers, so that margins become tighter, making increased income and profitability harder and harder. This scenario also creates a bureaucratic culture of recording costs in order to base price on them, and an obsession with cutting costs that may be counter to proper effectiveness and genuine improvement of the product or service offered.

Of course, cost-plus with a very small markup component will demonstrate all the above characteristics to a more restrictive degree than cost-plus with a more substantial or realistic markup.

Value-based pricing

Value-based pricing, by contrast with cost-plus, focuses on the potential benefits to the customer – what they're going to get, rather than what that is going to cost you. This pricing basis may be less appropriate where you're selling a fixed or standard commodity such as a simple widget, but in most cases of delivering products or services it is a far superior pricing strategy.

Value-based pricing involves in-depth awareness about how much your product or service adds to your customer's desired outcomes, benefits wished for or needs requiring fulfilling. For instance, if you were an accountant you could charge £2,000 to do someone's accounts for a year – or you could instead charge them 25 per cent of the tax you're saving them through your services. In this case, your pricing is based on the tangible value that you are delivering to the customer, and which they will be acutely aware of. Furthermore, the better your service, and the higher value you deliver to them, the more income you will generate.

Dyson, the manufacturer of revolutionary vacuum cleaners and other innovative household technology, is an excellent example of putting this latter principle into operation effectively. Dyson came into the market with something unique, and from the start based its pricing on the enhanced and indeed value they were bringing to the marketplace and to the customer – and continue to do so.

Bundle pricing

Bundle pricing involves pricing for a number of items at a time rather than just one. It's typically used to sell items that would naturally go along with an item you're already offering. This is a win–win for both customer and supplier. You can sell more to each customer, and at the same time reward them by giving them better prices or discounts for buying more. For instance, if you sell fishing rods at say £100, you could also bundle in a reel, fishing line, hooks, floats, sinkers and even bait; suddenly the customer can be spending £200 rather than £100. And overall, as you sell more items in one transaction, your gross profit margin and your net profit percentage for that transaction is going up.

Amazon are exploiting this approach when they inform you that 'People who bought this item also bought that item and also this other item.'

Premium pricing

Premium or *prestige pricing* involves positioning yourself to sell high-end goods or services, as do Rolls-Royce motors or Patek Philippe watches, as well as seven-star hotels – and, to a lesser degree, five-star hotels. You are then a high-end supplier; for people who buy in this category, price is not such an issue or not an issue at all.

However, establishing and maintaining a system of premium pricing in your business is heavily dependent on effective and distinctive branding and marketing, and it will usually take time and investment to build your reputation. You have to create in the prospect's mind a certain need that you can fulfil, and also the sense that they are buying the best in the marketplace. This is not an easy strategy to pursue, but it is highly profitable if you succeed.

However, even if you're not one of the Patek Philippes or Rolls-Royces of this world, you could still include a premium version or upmarket package as part of your offering, so that your customers have this option available. For instance, in the case above, you could include a fishing rod costing £500 instead of £100, for those top-end customers who only want the best. Your profitability will be higher on these items, even though you may sell less of them.

A specialised version of premium pricing is *skim pricing*. This is where you have a unique and highly competitive or market-leading product, but not much time to sell it, so you charge the maximum amount of profit per unit. Apple are masters at this – their products are time-sensitive because they bring out new versions that competitors will quickly imitate, and they are known for extremely high and reliable standards of product. So they put the product out, make a killing and quickly move on to the next upgrade or updated version, which they have already been working on for some time.

Loss leader pricing

Loss leader pricing involves selling your initial offering at an artificially lower price in order to 'get a foot in the door' – to penetrate the market and gain as many customers as possible. It's often employed by newcomers to a marketplace or to a new geographical location, and widely used competitively by supermarkets marking down a couple of basic items such as milk or bread, on the basis that customers will then buy other items while in-store.

This is a method widely used by bigger sellers, but can be appropriate for other businesses at certain stages in their development. It can work well if you are selling something inexpensively as a *hook*, and subsequently offer more profitable items to the customers you have attracted in this way.

Fixed project pricing

Fixed project pricing means setting a price for a whole project or service, rather than charging for individual components or by the hour. For instance, you might charge £5,000 or $8,000 to a business customer for setting up a software solution that they will then run themselves, rather than coming in serially and doing individualised one-off pieces of work.

This policy is becoming popular in service industries. Historically, service providers have priced by the hour, so that there has been no incentive for them to become efficient – if they spend more hours, they charge the customer more money. Clients can then perceive this as *ambush billing* – like accountants or solicitors who send a new bill each month, of an unpredictable amount. Clients generally prefer to know what the overall cost is going to be. They don't care how long the work takes – they want certainty – and fixed project pricing can deliver this. It also provides more certainty of income and planning for the deliverer of the service.

Retainer pricing

Retainer pricing means that the customer is charged an agreed amount over a period of time, such as a month or a year, which will cover whatever needs arise in that time. This, too, gives more certainty to the customer, and reliable income to the service provider. Sometimes the retainer level is based on paying actual costs up to an agreed maximum budget.

Conclusion

The pricing system or the combination of pricing options you choose will depend on many different factors. You might use one system for part of your offering and another system for a different component; or you might use different pricing options at different stages in your business development. My advice is to try different options and see which works best for you. Test your prices.

One size does not fit all, so if you're bringing something unique to the marketplace, your price should reflect your uniqueness.

People in business can get into a habit of thinking, 'What is the least amount of work I can do for every pound the customer spends with me?' This has become increasingly prevalent in the marketplace. My recommendation is to think instead, 'What is the maximum amount of value I can give to my customer for every pound they spend?' With this thinking, you will keep your customers for longer and they will also refer other customers to you.

But the real magic is that as you deliver more value, you can charge more because the customer sees higher perceived value. Then use the appropriate pricing system to deliver this – but value pricing has the edge here.

A number of other pricing forms are also sometimes used – please see shaznawaz.co.uk/pricingresources for more options.

5. Pricing and mindset

In this chapter, I'm going to tell you about:

- how people think and behave when they spend money
- why an understanding of this is absolutely crucial to your process of pricing
- and how to apply this understanding.

I'll show you what you should do, and what you should not do, in order to charge the right price for your service or product and so obtain the maximum return and increase in turnover and profit. I'll also show you how the way you think about your personal purchases could create immense difficulties in your own pricing strategy if you're not careful.

Why is mindset so important in pricing?

The key point about mindset and perception as they affect pricing is this: in most business settings, people will pay you according to how they perceive your business offering and your business to be – and this is the crucial bit – *based on their own emotions, feelings and perceptions*.

Someone who goes to Harrods in London automatically expects to pay more than they would at a less well-known or less prestigious retailer. This result has been achieved by Harrods based on many different criteria that they have deliberately developed, including:

- their name and their brand
- where they are situated
- how everything looks and feels
- their atmosphere and 'presence'
- their standard of quality
- the esteem in which they are held.

So the fundamental principle is this:

> How customers perceive you and your product to be = how they will respond to your price.

Heuristics

The science of investigating mindset is known as *heuristics* – studying the process in people's minds and how they think and behave – and in particular how they reach particular conclusions, judgements, decisions and choices. It's cognitive or mental psychology, applied in the everyday world.

So our concern here is all about how people make one particular decision or choice rather than another – choosing your product or service rather than a competitor's – and how this relates to pricing.

This whole aspect of how the individual's mind works is influenced by their:

- Knowledge
- Education
- Experience

- Expertise

- Upbringing

- Culture

- The people they interact with

All these factors affect how we think and how we behave – and how we buy.

Building a profile of your buyer

You need to build a profile of your ideal customer by factoring in all the points listed in the heuristics section on the previous page. To do this, you also need to answer a lot of other more specific questions about them, such as:

- What kind of car do they drive?

- What are their hobbies or pastimes?

- Which newspapers or magazines do they read?

- Where do they go on holiday?

Knowing all this about your ideal customer brings three immediate benefits:

- A good understanding of how they think.

- Clues on how to reach this customer and let them know about your offering.

- A good idea of how they buy. This can then help you to sell to them in the way that they buy as opposed to the way that you sell.

Buyers are not all the same

For instance, if someone drives a 7 Series BMW, flies business class, plays golf and holidays in the Bahamas, they will be a significantly different type of buyer from someone who drives a Ford, holidays in Tenerife and reads the *Sun* newspaper. These are two very different profiles. You absolutely need to know who your buyer is.

Once you know how particular people think, you can then target and market to them in the appropriate voice, and effectively engage with them.

For optimum pricing in particular, you want to know whether they are affluent or not, whether they are discerning and whether they are prepared to place higher than average value on distinctive features such as a high standard of customer care. This will very significantly affect how your business *is perceived to be* by them. You can then price and market accordingly.

You need to meet the expectations of your ideal client, based on their perceptions and their preferences – what they want their buying experience to be and what benefits they want it to bring for them. If we want a higher standard, and if we get it, then we certainly won't mind paying more for it – in fact we'll think of that as a natural part of making this kind of choice.

When will buyers pay more?

If people see value in what you're selling, and if they see it as helping them achieve their desired personal or professional outcomes in life, then they will pay more for it. For instance, if you're an accountant and you can demonstrate that you can improve a client's cash flow by saving them £20,000 in tax; and if the customer was formerly paying £5,000 and you charge 20 per cent more than that, then they won't mind paying the extra to you, because they're ending up achieving their desired outcome – increased income.

The principle is exactly the same for any business, with any product or service, in any industry – if you help people get what they want, they will not be so concerned about how much they pay for it.

Don't price too low

Another important factor in terms of buyer perception is that if something costs more we will generally expect it to be of superior quality – especially if it costs a *lot* more; think of the well-used sayings, 'You get what you pay for' and 'If it seems too good to be true, it probably isn't true.' If your price is too low, people will be sceptical about the quality and the outcomes your offering will help them to achieve.

A key element affecting perception is the credibility and reputation of the provider. If you're known for selling high quality goods, then your customers will positively expect your prices to be higher than your competitors, and will be cautious if they aren't. Virgin airlines are an example – they have a good reputation for offering a good service, so customers will naturally expect to pay more than they do on a no-frills airline.

How do *you* think about money and price?

Here's a thing. If you yourself are a 'price buyer' – someone who is always looking for the bargains and the cheap deals, and prioritising that over other considerations – and if you are trying to be a seller of premium products, then you will struggle with pricing. It will be harder for you to sell a premium product at a premium price, because you will be resistant to selling in the 'premium thinking' way, and there will be tell-tale signs of this that will affect your customer's belief that your product can meet their perceived needs.

You have to understand how *your customers* think. Just because *you* think this way doesn't mean that other people think the same way. This is a very common mistake in pricing and selling – and is disastrous.

Sell to the Sandras, not to the Cindys

Here's an example of two people who think about buying and price in these two very different ways. Let's say Sandra has bought a pair of shoes and is showing them to her friend Cindy. Cindy says, 'Wow, those are nice shoes, Sandra – how much did they cost?' and Sandra tells her they cost £300.

'I'd *never* pay that much for shoes,' says Cindy. Cindy has set aside the fact that she liked the shoes – she's now only concerned that they're not cheap shoes. Sandra saw value in the shoes that Cindy didn't. You the reader are almost certainly not now wearing the cheapest form of footwear that you could have purchased, because you perceived extra benefit or value in purchasing the footwear you *are* currently wearing – it might be the look, the comfort, or the brand name or cachet that they represent.

Very many sellers think, 'All my customers are price buyers, who want cheap'; this is an extremely commonplace attitude. But remember that not all your customers think this way, across the whole range of what they spend their money on. Think about one of your customers, even someone for whom economy is an important concern. Have they bought the cheapest car they could possibly have bought? Are they wearing only the most inexpensive clothes they could have chosen?

In practice, there are other determining factors as well as price for every single customer. If people didn't want extra value we just wouldn't have extremely successful high-end products such as those offered by Rolls-Royce and Bentley cars, Mont Blanc pens, Conqueror stationery or Apple products.

The right way to think about buying

The alternative to having a price buyer mentality is being a buyer who looks at added value based on perception and need – based on what you're *really* looking for. So the relevant question is always this: 'Is the extra value worth the extra payment?'

People value different things in different ways. If a person values their time highly, this will influence their buying decisions – someone who is training to run a marathon for their favourite charity but is very busy might buy a training machine to use at home, because that will save them time and enable them to fit the training into their busy schedule.

So people will absolutely pay more, depending on their particular needs, and their situation and circumstances. Trainers and consultants, for instance, know this. Someone who is going for an important career interview and has very poor interview skills or lack of confidence might be prepared to pay £1,000 for a session with a skilled consultant in this area, when they would normally pay a lot less for one-to-one coaching services. There are consultants in many fields who are very highly paid because they target customers with very particular and special or urgent needs that have a lot hanging on them.

What you need to do

So you need to think about – and become crystal clear about:

- who your customer really is
- how they buy
- what they buy

- their mindset: how they think and behave, their upbringing and education, the books and newspapers they read, their hobbies and pastimes, their political persuasion, what type of car they drive and so on

- their demographic: where they live, their age and gender, their income bracket and other such aspects.

You also need to be equally clear about the added benefits and value that you in particular offer in your particular service or product. Think about little things you could do to improve the perception surrounding your business and your offering. This might include:

- Customer service

- Personal service

- Aesthetic aspects of presentation

- Placement of your offering

- Staff uniforms or appearance

- Packaging, stationery, quality of carrier bags

Attention to detail in the buyer's whole experience is crucial in all such matters, as this is what most readily completes the buyer's assurance that you are a premium seller who can meet their precise needs. In fact the *buyer's experience* is becoming the single most important part of the process for the most progressive and highly successful businesses – experiential buying is the next big thing. Disney is a great example of this.

Conclusion

These are the key points never to forget about pricing perception:

- Don't underrate your offering; be proud of it

- If you don't value yourself, then no one else will either

- Just because you don't see value in something doesn't mean other people won't

- You don't know how somebody else makes a choice, so don't be presumptuous and try to second-guess it – methodically follow the processes set out in this chapter, and you will have a solid and reliable basis for your pricing strategy

- Make your product or service the very best that it can be, including all the matters of detail listed above

- It's not just your core product that counts, but everything else that goes with it; this is what distinguishes you and establishes your superior reputation

- Always have an added value offering in addition to your standard version – this will draw the discerning customer who will pay more

The only competition worthy of a wise man
is with himself.

Washington Allston

6. Pricing and competition

The question of competition between yourself and other players in the marketplace and the customers you're targeting is a key element in your overall pricing strategy.

Many people, when you bring up the subject of competition, think only of competing on price. But it's certainly not just a simple question of pricing lower than your competition – there's much more to it than that in terms of alternative approaches to increasing sales and winning business in a competitive field. The key aim is to position yourself competitively in your particular market – and that's certainly not just about having a competitively lower price.

Competing on price alone

Businesses who want to be competitively successful often compete simply on price – they want to be unambiguously cheaper than their competitors. I find again and again that this is seen as the best or indeed only way to quickly get lots of new customers. But this will very often not be appropriate for you, for a number of very good reasons. First of all, the competitor's product is likely to be different from yours in significant ways, and indeed may be inferior, so that you could end up offering a superior product at an equal or lower price.

Furthermore, routine competitive pricing in this way can simply involve you in a race to the bottom. What this means is that if you're reducing prices to get more customers, then it could end up being a never-ending price war. This usually leads to major cash flow issues or, at worst, bankruptcy. If you're an industry giant like Tesco then you can afford to have a price war due to economies of scale. A small business must avoid competing on price at all costs! It's very important that you consider this in the context of your margins in order to ensure that your business is profitable and therefore sustainable – that you can have a business for life, as opposed to always chasing the next customer. How to manage price in relation to margins is covered in more detail in Chapter 2.

Even with a somewhat standard product or service, in order to avoid competitively lower pricing you need to make your overall offering distinctive to differentiate it from others in the field, for instance by providing exceptional features or service, such as offering better after-sales service than your competitors. Rather than primarily competing on price, compete on differentiation, as the most successful businesses do.

Differentiation

Differentiation from your competitors can take many different forms, and presents numerous opportunities for a creative approach. If we look at any industry, we can see companies who successfully differentiated themselves, and the demise of others who didn't. Some years ago, for instance, the video rental chain Blockbuster was doing very well until a change in technology came about – the Internet was taking over from hard media like video cassettes and then DVDs. Blockbuster didn't do anything about it, and went belly up.

Netflix more recently observed that there was a change of behaviour and attitudes accompanying this development in home entertainment technology, and provided a distinctive service precisely to meet this need – and they are hugely successful, having a significant and highly influential disruptive effect on this lucrative marketplace. Many other disruptors have used differentiation, just like Netflix, to drastically change the marketplace. Well-known companies being Uber and Airbnb – and there are many more examples, who are all reaping rich rewards.

But more subtle forms of differentiation can be effected by other companies, including smaller ones. This is where you can offer something unique to your customers, which makes it difficult for them to compare you directly with others in your sector, so that they can't make a simple like-for-like comparison. John Lewis, for instance offers extended warranties. DFS offers interest free credit – spread over five years. Amazon Prime enables you to receive your purchase the very next day – and they're now working on using drone technology for delivery. You need to differentiate in a way that the market will appreciate, and will therefore be willing to pay more for.

Unique selling propositions

You can go further with this principle and develop a *unique selling proposition* (USP). Here we're talking about bringing something substantially different or distinctive to the marketplace and being competitive in that way, as opposed to simply differentiating something that is pretty much the same as others' offerings. Domino's exemplified this, announcing that they would deliver fresh, hot pizzas to your house in 20 minutes or less. Founder

Tom Monaghan thus arrived at a unique selling proposition that made him stand way out in his field. Such a USP represents a massive competitive and sustainable advantage in the marketplace. Dyson have done something analogous to this – and have kept doing so, over and over again.

What can you offer, then, which is distinctively different and is going to be appreciated by your customers? You have to, in the words of Apple founder Steve Jobs, 'think differently'. Ultimately this is not thinking outside the box – it's removing the box altogether. Get your team to come up with wild ideas for outrageous things you can do in this way, then look at how any of them can be turned into reality, even if they need to be toned down. Stretch yourself. Rather than imitating and being influenced all the time by what people are doing in your field, look at what is being done in other industries. Many professional groups such as accountants and lawyers only look at what other accountants or lawyers are doing. Then a disruptor comes along, makes a shedload of money – and then all the others imitate that person. Why not be the disruptor yourself?

Other measures to improve your competitive position

There are plenty of other alternatives to competitively low pricing as a means of selling more. Winning business by referrals is an extremely effective approach – other parties will in effect be doing your selling for you, and so you can spend less on marketing. Conversion rates are higher with referrals than with just about any other method of finding customers, which is why networking groups represent such a popular option today.

Another way to position yourself competitively in the marketplace is to develop ways of being seen as an authority in your field – so write blogs, articles, perhaps a book or create authoritative how-to videos on YouTube. Get authoritative stuff out there. As you educate people in these different ways, including giving them something for free so that they can see what you offer and experience the benefits, they will naturally come back to you for your products or services. And they will tell others.

You can carry this principle further. Be competitive by setting visibly high standards in how you do things, how you communicate, how you treat people – even down to details like what car you drive, what stationery you use, the pen you write with and how you speak. Show in all kinds of ways that you are a quality provider. As human beings, we're always passing judgement on others – as is often said, 'first impressions count'. Then people will see your offering as being of superior quality. Look like you're successful. Make yourself competitive with case studies and testimonials based on outcomes relevant to your preferred type of customer. These aspects of positioning are covered in further detail in Chapter 8. Offering guarantees or money back to customers who may not be fully satisfied are covered in Chapter 7.

Conclusion

All these strategies are preferable alternatives to simply competing on price, which has huge drawbacks – competing on price alone is generally only to be regarded as a last resort, the last option you would think about in a long list of competitive strategies that we have looked at in this chapter.

Look for something different about what you do and what you offer and how you offer it. If you're not going to be competitive and distinguish yourself in these ways, why should people buy from you? What's in it for them? Even if you're not a naturally competitive person, you can still think, all the time, 'How can I give people the best product or service and the best value, and give this benefit to the most people?' There's a huge amount you can do here, so I encourage you to be inventive, and go for it.

7. The power of guarantees

In this chapter I'm going to introduce you to the amazing power that a guarantee can have to attract more customers to your offering, and to enable you to become the go-to business that everyone chooses above your competitors.

I'm going to explain:

- the importance of guarantees and the principles on which they work
- what makes for a great guarantee
- the pitfalls to avoid
- the steps you need to take to design a viable, effective and profitable guarantee for your business and your products or services.

Making your offering stand out in the marketplace

In any marketplace, the competition is stiffer than most people think; so in order to stand out you have to be different. You have to distinguish yourself, and single yourself out from the competition in your field and your business environment. You have to think, 'How do I compel customers to buy from me rather than from one of my competitors?' That's the central issue.

Customers always discriminate – they are always thinking about where to spend their hard-earned money; they always want to get the maximum value from their investment. Customer discrimination is like comparing different kinds of fruit. It's easy to compare apples with other apples – the customer can easily tell which apples are the best and which apples represent the best value. But it's more difficult to compare apples with oranges. So if everyone in your marketplace is offering an apple, you need to think, 'How can I offer an orange, and therefore stand out?'

So how do you distinguish yourself, your company and your offering of a product or service?

The concept of the guarantee

A guarantee is an excellent way to do this because it demonstrates confidence in your offering, which inspires confidence and certainty in the customer. The customer naturally thinks, 'If this company is offering me a guarantee, then they must be pretty good at what they're doing.'

Furthermore, the guarantee represents a safety net for the customer – and customers like safety. If something goes wrong, the customers know that they can enforce the guarantee; so they are more confident and therefore more likely to buy from you – it's a no-brainer.

It's well known in sales psychology that we buy using emotion first – then we use logic to back up that emotionally based decision. We have a train of thought such as, 'What happens if I buy that lawnmower and it turns out not to cut grass very well, or if the blade gets blunt quickly, or maybe the whole thing will get rusty?… I'd better not buy this model.'

How much can I gain from offering a guarantee?

It's a big step to offer a guarantee on your service or product, but most businesses that are new to the concept are overly fearful, thinking that all their customers are going to ask for their money back. This is unlikely to be the case – the majority of customers will hopefully be satisfied if your offering is any good (if your offering isn't any good, then you've got a much bigger issue to worry about than pricing!), and not everyone who has a quibble about the purchase will take the trouble to follow up on a guarantee.

Let's look at the figures that justify offering a guarantee. If doing so increases your sales year on year by 10 per cent, and if 2 per cent of your customers ask for their money back, then you're still a lot better off. Table 2 shows how the figures work.

Table 2 The powerful effect of guarantees

			Scenario 1	Scenario 2	Scenario 3	Scenario 4
Increase in price			5%	10%	15%	15%
Refund rate			2%	4%	6%	10%
	From this year's results of	**To**	**Or**	**Or even**	**Or even**	
	£	£	£	£	£	£
Turnover	200,000		205,800	211,200	216,200	207,000
Costs	180,000		180,000	180,000	180,000	180,000
Misc. costs	20,000		25,800	31,200	36,200	27,000
	500		500	500	500	500
Profit improvement	£19,500		£25,300	£30,700	£35,700	£26,500
	29.74%		57.44%	83.08%	35.90%	

Examples of guarantees

Let's look at an example of a company that has used a guarantee to revolutionise the way they run their business, making big differences to their turnover, profit and market position.

Premier Inn hotels, owned by Whitbread, were ranked third in the UK hotel market in 2004 in terms of room revenue, but only had 3 per cent market share. Nine years later in 2013 they ranked first and had 12 per cent market share – an increase of 400 per cent (*Hotel Industry Magazine*, 2014). During this time they introduced a very strong guarantee, effectively saying, 'We're so confident that you'll have a good night's sleep here that if you don't, we will give you your money back.'

At an emotional level this guarantee is extremely comforting – nobody likes to be disturbed at night. So this guarantee was a coup in the marketplace and was a key element among the changes made that helped Premier Inn to massively improve their results. They plaster this guarantee all over their TV adverts and other media, including prominently on the sides of their supply lorries that are driven round the country. They are using this well-considered slogan to gain a huge competitive advantage.

The range of guarantee forms and types

A guarantee can be designed in a number of different forms, and it's important to choose the best type for your circumstances, and what you want to achieve with it.

- 100 per cent money back guarantee if the customer is not satisfied with the product or service, so that there is nothing for them to lose in making the purchase.

- Price match guarantee, so that the customer knows that they couldn't have made the purchase cheaper elsewhere.

- Risk-free period, for example, 30 days during which money back is guaranteed, so that the customer has time to try out the product and make sure that it meets their requirements and expectations.

- A guarantee often offered on serialised products such as magazine subscriptions involves the first issue or issues being supplied free; then payment is taken if the order is not cancelled.

- Enhanced or 'double' guarantees can also be offered: 'Buy our product, and if you aren't happy with it we will give you double your money back' or '… we will give you your money back plus an additional percentage'. This is used predominantly where marketing is extremely fierce. The option is more frequently offered in the US than in Europe.

Your action plan to produce a great guarantee

Here's a list of the essential questions you must ask yourself about your guarantee – the criteria that it must meet in order to be maximally successful.

- Is your guarantee clear and simple in terms of what it offers? Asterisks, 'read below' items and phrases such as 'terms and conditions apply' put people off.

- Does your guarantee embody genuine commitment to customer satisfaction? In other words: don't try to trick customers, otherwise the guarantee will have the opposite effect from what you intend. Terms such as 'cast-iron guarantee', 'no quibble' and 'no questions asked' encourage confidence in the customer's mind.

- Is your guarantee explicit and blatantly obvious in what it is offering? You need to believe in your guarantee, and commit to it. So there will be no small print get-out clauses or caveats to let you off the hook from fulfilling the guarantee if the customer is justified in claiming. Reasonable conditions are acceptable.

- Is it concise? Are there sections that are unnecessary, or that use too many words to explain the guarantee?

- Have you used precise language, so that the meaning can be accurately grasped by your customer, based on what is covered and the type of customer targeted?

- Is your guarantee more powerful than your competitors'? If your closest direct competitors are offering a price match guarantee, then you have to offer that plus something else on top, in order to have an impact; equalling a competing guarantee does not make you stand out.

A step-by-step guide to designing your perfect guarantee

1. Start by working out the three most important aspects of your product or service in terms of your customer's priorities, for example:

   o Quality

   o Performance

   o Standard of service

   o Speed of delivery

   o Other outcomes that are important to your customer

   You can determine these by talking to your customers and potential customers, and by looking at what other providers in your field are focusing on.

② Work out the weakest and least negatively impactful guarantee that you can think of, based on these customer satisfaction criteria – then turn this around into a strong guarantee. The idea is not to be ultra-brave, naive or extreme, but to find an appropriate level somewhere between the extremes. For example, look at Domino's Pizza: a weak guarantee would be 'to get the pizza to you as soon as we can' or 'to get the pizza to you within the hour'; the chosen guarantee is to deliver within 20 minutes. A guarantee like this seriously influences a customer's behaviour in your favour.

③ Theoretically test your guarantee. Work out its break-even point: the cost of paying out versus the cost of improving the quality of your offering in order to reduce payout.

To maximise the sales impact of your guarantee, test out the financial effect of different scenarios and how likely they are, such as:

o 2 per cent of your customers asking for a refund

o 5 per cent of your customers asking for a refund

o 10 per cent of your customers asking for a refund

Then add on the additional revenue brought in as a direct result of the guarantee. This will show you net impact based on initial calculations.

If the numbers don't add up, then carry out a small test to see if reality shows something different from your initial calculations. If it does, then great. If it doesn't, then look at changing the guarantee to make it stronger, so that more customers buy from you as a direct result.

④ Having arrived at your proposed guarantee terms, compare these with those of other players in your marketplace.

Being the first to offer a guarantee in a field where it's a viable option represents the ideal opportunity to become the market leader.

5. Test your guarantee: offer and publicise it specifically to new potential customers; see what happens, and how it effects sales and results. If you have a company that covers a very large area you could test in a single geographically limited zone, or you could test in the whole area with a limited range of products or services.

6. If the guarantee is not working optimally, ask yourself what is wrong. Check it against the list of essential questions above, then tweak or make changes accordingly, and retest on a limited basis.

7. If and when the guarantee is working optimally to your satisfaction, introduce it throughout the full intended business range or market areas.

8. Think about absolutely all the ways you can let potential customers know about your new guarantee, such as website, marketing and advertising materials, email signatures, press releases and by word of mouth. There's absolutely no point in offering a guarantee, then keeping it a secret.

9. Once the new guarantee is in place and widely publicised, increase your prices. When choosing between two products perceived as of equal value, customers will be prepared to pay a little more for the one with the better guarantee. Plus the peace of mind provided to them by the guarantee is an added-value benefit in itself.

Top tips for the perfect guarantee

These are the key points to bear in mind when designing and launching a guarantee:

- Show that you care
- Be honest
- Do what you promise in your guarantee
- Be courageous
- Make sure that the product or service covered by the guarantee is the best that it can be

Conclusion

You must remember at all costs that a guarantee is not a quick fix solution to make up for any deficiencies in your commercial offering. It's an integrated part of your whole approach to getting it to market.

So now go for it!

8. Positioning and pricing

Who you are in the marketplace is just as important as, if not more important than, what you're selling. Some people may refer to this as 'branding' – here, we're going to think of it as positioning. How you position yourself, your company and your product or service in relation to your potential customer and to your competitors is central to credibility and to pricing success.

We will talk here about a range of price-related strategies you can use to position yourself better in order to do more and better business. The most important aspects are:

- clarifying what your customer is getting in relation to the problem that will be solved for them by having your product or service

- giving the buyer significant choices and options

- demonstrating convincingly that your offering has worked for other customers.

The core of positioning strategy

Positioning is based most importantly on how your prospective customer perceives you: the more work you do in improving your positioning, the more likely your customers will be to see you as a market leader and view your offering as superior – which is the ideal position to aspire to. If you position yourself optimally, then you can get your optimum price and your optimum financial return. Branding, logos, website and marketing material packaging are some of the components that serve to support your positioning policy – but there's much more to it than that.

The process of pricing is all about presentation: how you position yourself and your product or service in the marketplace, and in relation to your potential customer.

Leading brands that have positioned themselves successfully to target a certain clientele will reap the rewards of comprehensively carrying through this strategy. The supermarket chain Aldi, for instance, is very clear on their ideal type of client, and accordingly they bear this client in mind when they think about the way they do everything, right down to the layout of their stores and the way staff behave. All these things provide clarity to the customer on what they are being offered, and how it relates to the marketplace. So you don't have to be the most expensive out there to implement this strategy – it can be done by any business, and *should* be done by every business.

Within the air travel industry, as another example, Ryanair and easyJet both position themselves as budget airlines that will get you from A to B as cheaply as possible, so if that's what you're looking for, then you know they will provide it. But even within this category, we can see the players endeavouring to position themselves relative to each other. Ryanair has added the option for passengers to carry on an extra hand baggage item, which can be a significant distinguishing feature that will appeal to a certain type of passenger.

The motor market demonstrates the power of positioning even more precisely, in an industry where positioning is crucial to customer decisions about spending a substantial amount of money. Volvo positions itself on safety – they've managed to make sure that when you think safety, you think Volvo. All their models are built around this primary positioning. Toyota is positioned around reliability. Ferrari is about looks, speed and affluence. Audi is about technical merit.

Skoda is an interesting example of a company that has changed its positioning, to great advantage. It was a poor person's brand 30 years ago. When I was young, if your parents drove a Skoda, you'd get them to drop you off at the end of the road rather than at the school, otherwise you would get a hard time from other pupils. Now, Skoda is seen as the most reliable car you can find – yet also economical to run and affordable to buy. This is why many taxi ranks around the world are filled with Skodas. Positioning.

Know your customer

Having a clear idea of your ideal customer profile is crucial to successful positioning. A majority of the companies I help will tell me that their ideal client is 'Everybody!' But this is not true, because every company is going to be offering *something* unique and different, which will be attractive to a particular type of clientele. So you need to work out exactly who that clientele is, for you and your business.

The watchmaking company Audemars Piguet is a good example of doing this well. If you do a web search for their name, the first two watches you see will be priced around £55,000 to £70,000. They are very clear on who their clientele is, and everything they do is targeted at this clientele, in terms of marketing message, advertising, branding and the product itself. Their watches are certainly not cheap, and that is a key part of their positioning strategy – they use it as an advantage. However, this principle is not important only for the top tier of companies with expensive and exclusive products. It's important for you, too.

Credibility is crucial in this, as much so for downmarket offerings as for the top charging companies. Your credibility is dependent upon how much trust you have built up. You gain trust by how you behave, and how you are perceived by the client – the information you share with people, whether you have their best interests at heart, your service, and aftercare and ongoing servicing if appropriate. Every customer will want to know: do these people do what they say, and deliver on what they say they will do, and are their claims credible? Do I believe what they are telling me? All that links to trust – we only believe somebody if we trust them.

So this is partly about how credible your product or service is, how credible you are as a company – and how credible you and your staff are as people.

Personal positioning

Personal positioning is an important aspect of the overall positioning of what you offer in the marketplace, and is equally bound up with the issue of pricing strategy. It's all about how you are personally seen, and how you come across to your customers and prospects.

For instance, if you have a secretary or personal assistant who answers the telephone for you, this will generally elevate the customer's idea of your position, compared to answering the phone yourself – although customers calling mobile numbers will expect you to pick up personally. Even though people like accessibility to the company they're dealing with, they will think more highly of you if they have to jump over hurdles in order to speak with you directly – so they will expect to pay more for that quality.

Customers will be similarly influenced by other aspects of personal positioning, such as:

- How well you dress, as well as details such as your watch and the pen you use
- What car you drive
- The appearance of your premises
- The company stationery, and indeed all your paperwork, especially photographs that show what you look like
- The impression created by your website and other online presence
- The company you keep, and the people you know and mention (especially so in the US)

If these all create an impression of high quality, then the customer will generally think you are better than a competitor who fails to create an impression which demonstrates high quality. It's all about the widely recognised power of association – associated qualities will be consciously or unconsciously transferred from how you are personally to what you are offering. In other words, how you do one thing will be seen by others to infer how you do everything.

The actual implications can vary somewhat in practice according to what kind of market and what type of customer you're targeting. For instance, if you're looking for customers who are not so well off, you might not want to present such an upmarket personal impression, or people might resent knowing what you've spent their scant and hard-earned cash on. One of my clients told me of a big customer who happened to see him parking his Porsche, and immediately cancelled the long-term order. But generally, the best option will be to do everything you can to elevate your position. In some countries, including the UK, people in business are hesitant to do this, and that can work against you because of the corresponding assumptions people will be making about you and what you're offering.

Authoritative positioning and social proof

Social proof is the name given to evidence you can provide to your potential customers to demonstrate that you have authoritative and superior positioning in the marketplace. So the fundamental trust you are seeking to build can be reinforced by this social proof.

In the marketplace, most people don't want to bad-mouth a supplier because it reflects badly on them, and nobody wants to be seen as a foolish person who bought something that doesn't work or is very bad value. Fear of this happening leads to caution in potential buyers: they hold back on the step of making the purchase.

Confidence in a potential buyer, on the other hand, leads to more sense of certainty and increased likelihood of taking the next step and committing to a purchase.

So if you can demonstrate that your product or service has worked for someone else, buyers are likely to believe that it will work for them, reducing their sense of risk of being let down or wasting money.

Examples include weight loss programmes that show before-and-after photos of successful slimmers, reviews of restaurants or hotels such as on TripAdvisor, Amazon reader ratings, or

QVC-style TV channels demonstrating the power of a blender by tossing an iPhone into it and the blender still working fine.

If you can establish your ideal client's profile, and project this so that it comes through in all aspects of your business presentation, then other potential customers will think, 'Those people are like me, and they have bought this product; so if they believe in this offering, then I can believe in it too.'

So if you can demonstrate convincingly that what you are selling works, more people will buy. Testimonials work very well, if they show what the problem was, how it was solved and how things are now – and provide credible details from the person providing the testimonial and their business that are relevant to your potential customers. Booking.com, TripAdvisor, Trustpilot and others have shown this – people won't believe what we say about ourselves as we're biased, but they will believe what other people say; this is taken as real proof.

Testimonials must be set up appropriately, however. They need to be up to date, not five years old – they should be fresh, relevant and current. Using your existing testimonials for the next ten years is no good – and anyway, you're probably better now than you were then. And if you have lots of testimonials from customers who are 70 years old, a 20 year old is not going to be convinced. It's all about demographics. Get Google reviews for your business, too – this will help to make you stand out. Go crazy on this point; get as much as you can in the way of social proof.

If a customer has to choose between two similar services, one of which has such reviews and the other hasn't, they are highly likely to buy from the former. Celebrity endorsement is particularly persuasive, if you can get it.

You can expand on the principle of offering testimonials on your website or marketing materials, by offering to put new potential customers in touch with existing customer advocates who have agreed to be contacted for evaluation of your services.

Positioning through price expression

How you state price is influential, and can have an effect on positioning in the marketplace. This has been studied in-depth, and it appears that the numbers 99, 97 or 47 and similar numbers ending with 7 can be used in order to seem less expensive. But things are changing as the buyer becomes more aware. £4.99 can seem cheaper than £5.00, but can now sometimes also be seen as a cynical ploy, with a negative effect, whereas £4.97 is not.

Another approach is to chunk the price down so that it doesn't sound so daunting to the spender, which works for some types or product or service. For instance, £182.50 per year could be stated as 50p per day, putting the outlay into perspective: 'Less than a cup of tea per day' can feel more affordable to most people – if this works for your ideal client. Items such as sports club membership are often stated monthly rather than as an annual sum.

Double glazing and window replacement has historically made this presentation of pricing an art form – first they hit you with a higher price, then they talk about a big discount. Some businesses still do this; well-known furniture retail stores always have a sale on throughout the year. Even though we catch on to it, and we know it's not a genuine sale or genuine reductions, they still keep doing it, so it must work. People still buy stuff from them.

Giving the buyer options is persuasive, such as offering tiered pricing structures: 'good option/better option/best option' or 'bronze/silver/gold' – adding something extra that will be valued at each level such as warranty, replacement or other add-ons.

It's hugely valuable to compare what the customer is getting with the problem that will be solved for them by having your product or service. This is known as the *contrast* principle, and is at the core of selling anything to anyone. For instance, show the customer that an existing situation or issue is costing them £xxx or $yyy, and then set this against what you will charge to remove that problem. This is known as the *framing* or *anchoring* approach to presenting price.

Conclusion

So I encourage you to think and rethink about all these aspects of the positioning of yourself, of your company and of the product or the service that you're offering, in relation to the expectations and the aspirations of your ideal customer, and their impression of how your offering can make their lives better.

Life is dangerous. There are no guarantees.

RuPaul

Reading list

Ariely, D. (2009) *Predictably Irrational: The hidden forces that shape our decisions*. HarperCollins.

Baker, R.J. (2006) *Pricing on Purpose: Creating and capturing value.* John Wiley & Sons.

Cialdini, R.B., Ph.D. (2007) *Influence: The psychology of persuasion.* HarperBusiness.

Cram, T. (2005) *Smarter Pricing: How to capture more value in your market.* Financial Times/Prentice Hall.

Hotel Industry Magazine. (2014) 'Premier Inn: From strength to strength.' 8 September. Available at: http://www.hotel-industry.co.uk/2014/09/premier-inn-from-strength-to-strength/

Joyner, M. (2005) *The Irresistible Offer: How to sell your product or service in 3 seconds or less*. John Wiley & Sons.

Kennedy, D.A. (2011) *No B.S. Price Strategy: The ultimate no holds barred kick butt take no prisoner guide to profits, power, and prosperity*. Entrepreneur Press.

When you're in a position to have gotten so much, the gift at this point is giving back.

Paul Stanley

About the author

Shaz Nawaz BA MA ACA is a financial consultant with particular expertise in pricing strategy. He runs four businesses of his own.

He has conducted 3,000+ business growth consultations and led thousands of businesses to greater growth and profit – and guidance on pricing has been crucial in most cases. Thousands of his clients have increased their prices and profits, in all sectors. His presentations and seminars on the subject of pricing strategy are in high demand.

Having started out as a chartered accountant, Shaz has also worked as an investment accountant at J.P.Morgan investment bank. He has received a number of awards including The World's Most Inspiring Accountant.

Leadership is a mindset in action. So don't wait for the title. Leadership isn't something that anyone can give you. You have to earn it and claim it for yourself.

Travis Bradberry

Other Authority Guides

The Authority Guide to
Trusted Selling:
Building stronger, deeper, more profitable
relationships with your customers to
create lifetime loyalty

Paul Avins

**Do you want to build more profitable relationships with your
customers?**

In today's volatile world sales professionals must know how to build trust
in their company, their products and ultimately themselves in order to win
the business. In this *Authority Guide*, sales coach Paul Avins shares his
proven 4-step system to help you contact, connect and convert more
customers with less effort and no pressure.

The Authority Guide to Networking for Business Growth: How to master confident, effective networking and win more business

Rob Brown

You can master the mysterious art of networking.

Overcome all your networking fears and learn how effortlessly to build leverage and the powerful connections you need to enhance your reputation, raise your profile and win more business. Networking expert Rob Brown will coach you on all the essential skills that will help you meet new people, create new leads, open up opportunities and grow your business – confidently and effectively.

The Authority Guide to Practical Mindfulness:
How to improve your productivity, creativity and focus by slowing down for just 10 minutes a day

Tom Evans

Enhance your wellbeing, creativity and vitality with mindfulness meditation.

In this *Authority Guide*, Tom Evans, invites you to embrace the benefits of meditation in both your life and your business. With the practical mindfulness meditative techniques described in this book, you will learn how to get more done in less time. You will discover how to generate ideas off the top of your head and how to allow serendipity to land at your feet. This book opens the door to a new way to be and do.

The Authority Guide to Engaging Your People:
Raise staff performance and wellbeing, increase profitability and improve customer satisfaction

Sue Mitchell

Engagement helps business to be more resilient and succeed through periods of change.

This *Authority Guide* addresses how businesses can increase their performance, productivity and customer/staff satisfaction through focusing on engagement. Sue Mitchell, an authority in coaching and leadership development, shows you how to build a team who is committed, inspired and eager to deliver their best work in order to make a difference.

The Authority Guide to Meaningful Success:
How to combine purpose, passion and promise to create profit for your business

Tim Johnson

Business results and meaningful work connect to impact effectiveness in our organisations and lives.

Tim Johnson, founder of Meaningful Success, shows you how to integrate practical business thinking with practical personal development to create global impact through your business or charity. This *Authority Guide* blueprints how we can embrace the best elements of entrepreneurial drive and passion, and an enabling blame-free culture to lead high-performing teams whilst providing personal fulfilment for all.

The Authority Guide to Writing & Implementing a Marketing Plan: Critical steps to create maximum profits for your business

Ambrose and Jo Blowfield

Have a sales plan? Now you need a marketing plan.

Written especially for small businesses, this *Authority Guide* shows you how to write and execute your marketing plans efficiently and accurately. Ambrose and Jo Blowfield will help you create a plan using proven, affordable marketing tactics for both digital and traditional strategies. You'll have a year long marketing plan that is structured, well thought out and targeted to your ideal clients, allowing you proactively to promote your business.

The Authority Guide to Financial Forecasting for SMEs: Pain-free financials for finance and planning

Simon Thompson

Build a better, faster forecast.

In this *Authority Guide*, forecasting guru Simon Thompson shows you how to build financial forecasts quickly, effectively and cheaply through his unique, proven and easy-to-follow 10-step process. By learning how to create effective forecasts you will master the ability to understand the potential financial outcomes for your business and be able to communicate financial information in order to successfully raise investment or loans.

The Authority Guide to Emotional Resilience in Business: Strategies to manage stress and weather storms in the workplace

Robin Hills

How do your challenges inside and outside of work impact upon your emotions and your resilience?

The emotional resilience of those involved in a business will contribute significantly to the organisation's success. This *Authority Guide* from leading emotional intelligence expert, Robin Hills, will help you change the way you think about yourself and the way you approach potentially difficult situations. You will be able to develop your own personal resilience and understand how to develop resilience within the hearts and minds of your team and your organisation.

The Authority Guide to Developing High-performance Teams: How to develop brilliant teams and reap the rich rewards of effective collaboration in the workplace

Andrew Jenkins

Are you making the most of the greatest asset in your business?

To make your good business a great business you need to have more than just a strong product or service. Having a high-performing team in your organisation is guaranteed to give you a competitive advantage. Andrew Jenkins helps you discover how to cultivate in your people the willingness to grow as individuals and as a group. Packed with easy-to-follow activities, exercises and models, this *Authority Guide* explains how to build a high-performing, collaborative, trusting and resilient team.

We hope that you've enjoyed reading this *Authority Guide*. Titles in this series are designed to offer highly practical and easily-accessible advice on a range of business, leadership and management issues.

We're always looking for new authors. If you're an expert in your field and are interested in working with us, we'd be delighted to hear from you. Please contact us at commissioning@suerichardson.co.uk and tell us about your idea for an *Authority Guide*.